To all of the people who gave me life:

Arnold Palmer Hospital where I spent my childhood
Anne who is my second mom
Dr. Ramirez who is practically my dad
My Mom who is my best friend
My actual best friend Bryce, who accepts my uniqueness
Nonni & Grandpa who taught me to always stay hungry for knowledge
and Vincent Izzi who has guided me in all of my business endeavors.

And to my sweetest Olive
who always brightens my day
and now gets to brighten the days of others.

You never know how **strong** you are,
until being **strong** is your only option.

- Bob Marley

Copyright © 2019 by Makenzie Morgan LLC

All rights reserved.
No part of this publication may be reproduced, distributed,
or transmitted in any form or by any means, including photocopying,
recording, or other electronic or mechanical methods, without the prior
written permission of the publisher, except in the case of brief quotations
embodied in critical reviews and certain other noncommercial uses
permitted by copyright law. For permission requests, write to the publisher,
addressed "Attention: Permissions Coordinator," at the address below.

Makenzie Morgan LLC
16301 Innovation Lane
Fort Myers, FL 33913
www.MakenzieMorgan.org

Ordering Information:
Quantity sales. Special discounts are available on quantity purchases by
corporations, associations, and others.
For details, contact the publisher at the address above.
Orders by U.S. trade bookstores and wholesalers.
Please contact IngramSpark: visit www.ingramspark.com.

Printed in the United States of America

Hardback ISBN: 978-1-7336030-0-3
Paperback ISBN: 978-1-7336030-3-4
Ebook ISBN: 978-1-7336030-1-0

First Edition

Meet Olive!

She is a happy little pig, who loves to go to school, play with friends, and eat lots of fruit!

When Mommy and Olive arrived at the hospital, it looked so scary from the outside, but on the inside, it wasn't scary at all!

Olive got to play all kinds of games while waiting.

There were *puzzles*,
coloring,
and *electronic games*.

"Olive, the doctor is ready to see you!" the nurse called and Mommy and Olive followed her from the waiting room and down the hallway.

The nurse asked Olive to stick out her tongue
and she put a thermometer under it
to get her temperature.

Next, the nurse asked Olive to take
her shoes off and stand on a scale to measure
how much she weighed and how tall she was.

Then, she put a cuff around her arm to
measure Olive's blood pressure. The cuff
squeezed her arm until it fell asleep!

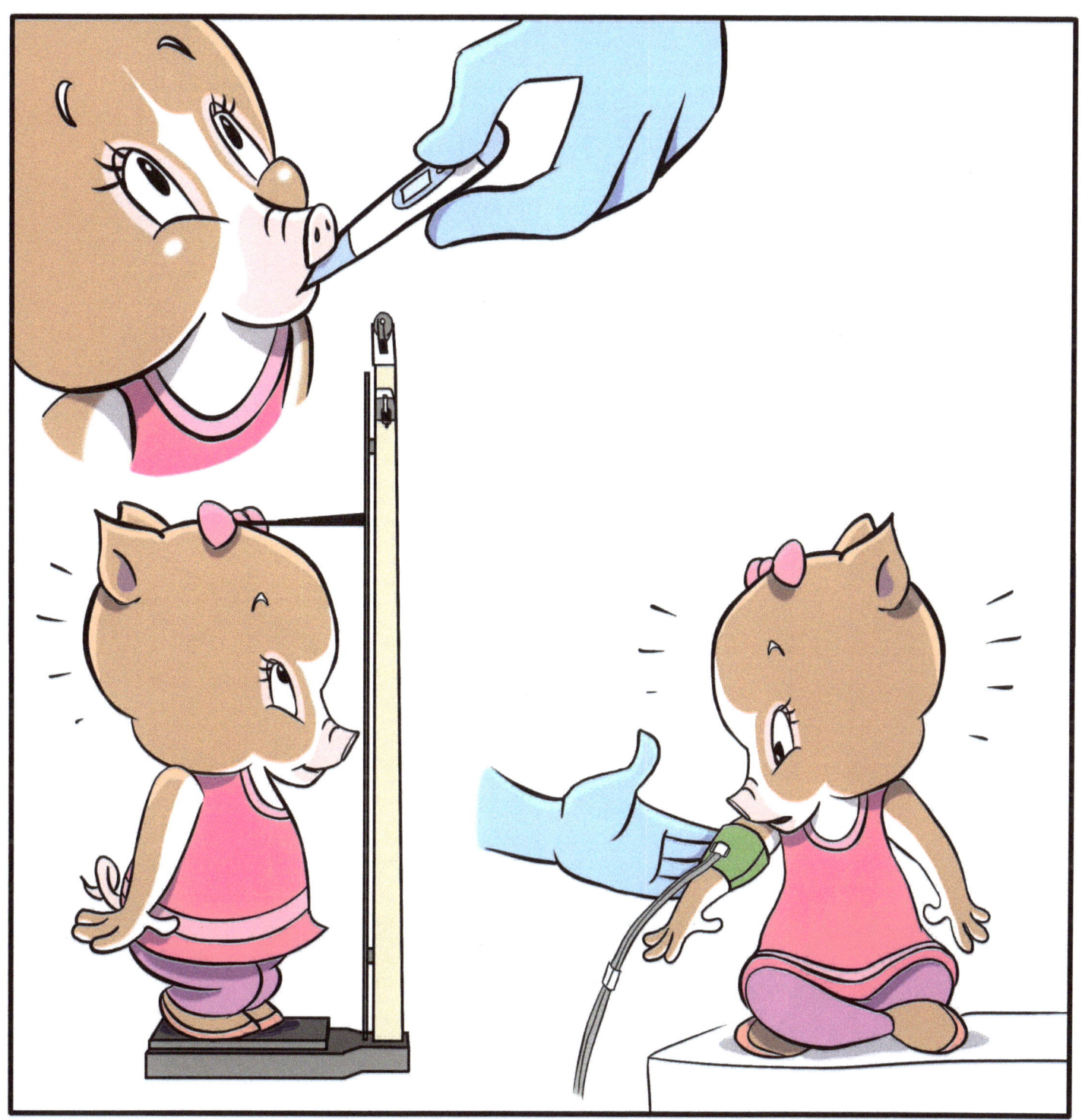

Finally, the nurse gave a little cup to Mommy and asked her to help Olive go pee in it in the restroom. After they finished, Mommy gave the cup back to the nurse and she put a little piece of paper in it that changed colors!

The doctor instructed Mommy to take Olive to the top floor of the hospital, so they went up the elevator. When the doors opened to the kid's kidney center, Olive noticed that it looked like they were in the sky!

Mommy and Olive went to another examination room and waited for the kidney doctor.

While they waited, a new nurse came in and told Olive that she needed to test her blood. She used a tiny needle that looked like a butterfly and told Olive that it would be a tiny prick in her arm. The nurse counted,

"One...
　　Two...
　　　　Three..."

Bright red blood quickly filled into little tubes and after she was done, Olive got to pick out a Band-Aid!

The nurse left with Olive's blood and Mommy and Olive kept waiting for the doctor in their exam room.

The doctor's office gave Olive some stickers for behaving so well, and Mommy took her to the store to pick out a toy.

Olive picked out a stuffed toy that looked just like her and they headed home.

After Olive ate her favorite dinner, she watched some television with Mommy.

Mommy told Olive it was time for bed, so they went upstairs and Mommy tucked Olive in.

"Even though you were scared, you were so brave today," Mommy said as she kissed Olive's forehead, "I am so proud of you."

Sources and Resources

Living Well with Kidney Disease by the National Kidney Foundation of Southern California
ISBN: 978-0-9700593-1-4

www.kidney.org   National Kidney Foundation

www.kidneyfl.org   National Kidney Foundation of Florida

www.nephcure.org   NephCure Kidney International

www.arnoldpalmerhospital.com/pediatric-specialties/pediatric-nephrology
Arnold Palmer Hospital for Children - Hewell Kids Kidney Center

www.donatelife.net   Donate Life America

Terms You May Need to Know

Acute: Acute often means urgent. An acute disease happens suddenly. It lasts a short time. Acute is the opposite of chronic, or long lasting

Chronic: Lasting a long time. Chronic diseases develop slowly. Opposite of Acute

Creatinine: A waste product from meat protein in the diet and is a by-product of normal muscle metabolism. It can be tested in your blood to measure how well your kidneys remove wastes from your body.

End-Stage Renal Disease (ESRD): the same meaning as the term 'chronic kidney disease', 'stage 5', or the stage of kidney damage that requires dialysis or kidney transplantation

Focal Segmental Glomerulosclerosis (FSGS): a rare disease that attacks the kidney's filtering units

Glomular Filtration Rate (GFR): a blood test that indicates at what rate the kidneys are filtering the blood

Kidneys: the 2 bean-shaped organs that filter wastes from the blood. They are located near the middle of the back. They create urine

Nephrologist: refers to a doctor who is primarily concerned with the medical treatment of patients with kidney disease or kidney failure

Nephrology: scientific study of kidneys

Nephrotic Syndrome: a collection of symptoms that include lots of protein in the urine, low blood proteins, and body swelling.

Polycystic Kidney Disease (PKD): an inherited disorder characterized by many grape-like cysts that make the kidneys larger over time and destroy tissue

Renal: refers to the kidneys

Renal Cell Carcinoma: a type of kidney cancer

Renal Osteodystrophy: weak bones caused by poorly working kidneys

Meet Makenzie & Olive!

Author Bio: Throughout Makenzie's struggles with kidney disease, she prides herself on giving back to her community. Since she was young, she has spoken for Arnold Palmer Hospital for Children, the National Kidney Foundation, and Children's Miracle Network of Greater Orlando to help raise money to give other children the resources that she didn't have, like the Hewell Kids Kidney Center in Arnold Palmer Hospital for Children. Now, she still works with those non-profits, while expanding to others in Southwest Florida, after moving to Fort Myers to attend Florida Gulf Coast University. She is now a senior majoring in English, with minors in Creative Writng and Entrepreneurship in hopes of reaching even more children throughout the country with chronic illnesses.

Makenzie's Kidney Journey: At the age of 2, Makenzie was diagnosed with Focal Segmental Glomerulosclerosis (FSGS) and Nephrotic Syndrome. Upon the age of 6, she went on peritoneal dialysis every night for 14 hours. On her 7th birthday, she got one of her biological kidneys removed. Three months later, in hopes of being ready for transplant, she got her other biological kidney removed. After another month, her body and donor were ready and she received her transplant on October 22nd, 2004. Ten wonderful went by and at the beginning of her senior year in high school, she went to her nephrologist to get him to sign off on joining her school's swim team. After getting blood work done 4 weeks early from stopping in, she discovered she was in a chronic kidney rejection.
After 2 years of IVIG infusions, Rituximab (chemotherapy), biopsies, and heavy steroids, she lost a lot of kidney function, but has been able to live with the same kidney today.

Olive's Bio: Olive is a 2-year-old Juliana/American Mini Pig mix, who was born in the panhandle of Florida. She lives with her mom, Makenzie, in Southwest Florida. She loves all kinds of fruits and vegetables, and she loves to lay out in the sun! She is full grown at 40lbs and is about the size/weight of a medium dog. She knows how to use a litter box, sit, spin around, and walk on a leash! She loves to meet other animals and people and she makes all kinds of sounds to talk to you!

You can follow Olive on Instagram!   @olive_themini

Check out more products and stories below!

Website:
www.MakenzieMorgan.org

Facebook Page:
www.facebook.com/writerMakenzieMorgan/

Instagram:
@Writer_MakenzieMorgan

Olive's Instagram:
@Olive_themini

www.ingramcontent.com/pod-product-compliance
Lightning Source LLC
Chambersburg PA
CBHW061129070526
44584CB00033B/4274